Seeking
the
Button Rock Hermit

Tony Burfield

Seeking the Button Rock Hermit
© Tony Burfield 2022

No part of this book may be reproduced by any means known at this time or derived henceforth without written permission of the publisher or author. The exception would be in the case of brief quotations embodied in the critical articles or reviews and pages where permission is specifically granted by the publisher or author.

Books may be purchased in quantity and/or special sales by contacting the publisher. All inquiries related to such matters should be addressed to:

Middle Creek Publishing & Audio
9161 Pueblo Mountain Park Road
Beulah, CO 81023

editor@middlecreekpublishing.com
(719) 369-9050

First Paperback Edition, 2022
ISBN: 9781957483047

Cover Design: David Anthony Martin
Cover Image art image courtesy USGS 1962 Rattlesnake Reservoir

Printed in the United States

Seeking
the
Button Rock Hermit

Tony Burfield

Middle Creek Publishing
Beulah, CO USA

Table of Contents

Proper Field Notes..................................13
Hermit Tracking.. 31
Dear Hummingbird........................... 49
Hiding Hermit.. 69

In memoriam of Scott King
Naturalist, Poet, Editor, Printer

Seeking the Hermit

Trying to find Button Rock, itself, is challenging enough—let alone the Button Rock Hermit. Readers familiar with the Button Rock Preserve between Lyons, Colorado and Estes Park know this. At the preserve, one finds the Button Rock Trailhead, but this trail does not lead to Button Rock, nor Button Rock Mountain. In fact, Button Rock is not even on the actual mountain. Instead, the rock itself is its own peak, sitting just east and slightly to the north of the mountain that shares the name. To make matters even more perplexing, numerous "button rocks" can be found all through this area. Boulders and large slabs of rock—some the size of a warehouse and bigger—seem to have pushed themselves up through a seam in a forest or meadow and now sit on top, like a button. Perhaps this is one reason for the profusion of button rock naming in the area. It is not too hard to imagine two hikers both talking about having found "button rock" yet speaking about two totally different places.

And so, when one turns to the cover of *Seeking the Button Rock Hermit*, they find a map. A trickster map. A map that seems to locate Button Rock with effortless ease. And yet, even when one finds Button Rock, they have not yet found the Button Rock Hermit. What kind of map can lead one to *her* dwelling place?

Tony Burfield provides one kind of map through his elusive poetics of naming. Poem after poem follows prints, scat, and scents leading both the speaker and the reader into brush encounters with the hermit. However, the speaker of the poem may shift through a plural pronoun, starting as human, becoming animal. Or lichen. Or rock. Not unlike the shapeshifting hermit. After all, a track or a trace is simply a mark on the earth. It is something tangible like a bone or a tuft of fur, but it points toward something that is elusive. No longer there. Absent.

The first poem establishes the elusive poetics of naming, and each poem that follows continues the journey of the search. Burfield works through haibun, a poetic form made up of three parts: a title, a section of prose, and a section of haiku. As a reader journeys through the collection, a meditative space opens up.

In an early poem, the speaker feels his *"own off-tip step"* moving *"each step after a little to the left."* This line ends the prose section of the poem before turning toward haiku and toward a solidarity with nonhuman ways of being: *"rhythm / in junco flit / Balance."* And it's the *off-tip balance* of the three-part haibun that buoys up the reader, that mesmerizes the reader, that leads the reader into the mythic, elusive encounters with Earth.

These encounters are, as mentioned, mythic, but they are also grounded within the flora and fauna of the mountains. The precision of the naming of plants and animals, their tracks and traces, leads one toward a sense of deep solidarity with innumerable species of this shared planet. This generates a sense of overlapping human, plant, and animal communities. And yet, such communities are in tension with the "sacred loneliness" of the solitary search for the mythic hermit. The search grants readers a greater awareness of being within a tiny, little sliver of the planet—a way of being that celebrates, seeks, mourns, and grapples with existential questions including how to seek the hermit given today's planetary ache.

Seeking the Button Rock Hermit is most definitely grounded in a specific place. But the method of the search speaks to any reader looking to reclaim or deepen one's mythic experience of the Earth. In an age when the Earth is so often anything but sacred, Burfield follows a scent and finds a "fox trail" worth tracing especially as it leads *"seemingly right off // the cliff"* into what we will never know or grasp. Such a poetics pushes us to the limits of what we can grasp, and perhaps just beyond for a moment, until the tatter we follow vanishes a little further out than we thought we could reach.

—Aaron M. Moe,
 author of *exhalations*, and *Ecocriticism and the Poiesis of Form*

Proper Field Notes

Hermit Naming

The Button Rock Hermit has had many names. She was once called the Woman of the Woods; the old timers called her the Vixen; she was known as the Brush Shaker, the Grackle, the Rootress, the Mountain Ghost, and on and on. We think now that she lives in Sister Rain Cave, but it is said she was born on top of Button Rock and that her great, great grandmother was also called the Button Rock Hermit. Although, she might also be the one who paints the forest red with blood.

big pile
of cougar scat —
they dance, jig

Chasing Summer

Proper field notes. The Button Rock Hermit sun-facing. Tiny yellow birds, tipping the grass leaves so slightly and on their backs, a black cloak. They're headed south they say, headed for warmer forests before the first freeze. And the late sky, deep grey cloud and blue, that hard autumn blue, seeping back in. We walked and got hot. The steep mountain dirt roads keep us guessing at which gods are to the north.

smart sunflower
your logic-turn flawless
under photon arch

Scat Identification

Today we identify as coyote
the place of tooth and tongue
and duff snout
the body of perfect yowl
the evening wildfire smoke
lingering and we try at bone
crush.

Recluse parsing
our scat.

Close to the Feeder

Some blue-purple sky and drops on wind. I walked the Deer Loop tonight and ran into the neighbor, Jackie, a Texan and tall. She had binoculars and was spying on a grockle who had parked a camper on her land. "I've called the sheriff 'cause I don't want a fight … the rufous are thick this time of year. I can get them to land on my finger, close to the feeder." Then her dog, Bella, came up with her blue-purple eyes.

ants lined-up
on the hummingbird feeder
tourist traffic

Tomato Dusk

We count the tomatoes red and green. And the yard yucca roll-call. The deer have eaten all the stalk tips. I deconstruct the old grill to build a table for the outside work, for saws and nails, those hammers, my work gloves. Beside my sweat and tools, traffic surges in leaf-peeper ecstasy and the motorcyclists die in droves. The highway crosses pile-up in memoriam, cruxifixal road bones. And with these tomatoes we christen the summer dead too, all tools rusted.

dry fox jaw sun
baked all summer —
tomato dusk

Canid Minutes

Scratch it out. Out there in the freezing fog, night in wolf time, the coyote yaps and the beta-vixen screams. We tumble on each other, inside and warm. We rake our leaf collections into intricate art piles. All our friends have left somewhere to cities, but out there in tooth time the canids scratch, the canids steam.

dog years
stretching in the sun
a single howl

Hoarfrost Complexities

Hoarfrost long thin. Hoarfrost thick squat. Hoarfrost tongue sharp in straight sunlight. My presence is violence to pine squirrels. Their barks do echo, corvid calls too. As I climb through gully and gulch, over icy boulders and across the hand-built 2x4 bridge creaking, I feel my own off-tip step. Each step after a little to the left.

rhythm
in junco flit
Balance

Reptilian Brain

The point from which, my dear, we can see the Mummy Range. My connect. Our lips on hoarfrost pine. A tangle of chickadees but there's something in the woods, something quiet and loud. We listen to an unknown bird sound alarm. I say, "Someone else on the mountain." You say, "It's quiet." I push my hiking stick into the duff and hear a deep barrel grunt from above in the boulders. "We should go down."

wet scents
on top the old snow
our reptilian brains

The Rut

It's ritual that mixes the concrete. Our ritual is our vein to cosmos. Our rut. It tilts the pen, salt-washes the paper, sets the recurve stance. And these visions transmogrify our rites, she with hand-stitched feathers and my ink scratches. We're toothed in this mountain valley, I'm c-walk and she's two-step swagger, our physical intelligences enough for quorum. We twine and barrel. The ritual of ink and thought, of seconds spread through youth and age. And the muscle fibers around my knee joints buzz in anticipation of tomorrow's cliff-up frog hop.

pen here
book there
evening tea

Good Life

It's always forever. Sunny, cool, fall day. All blue-black now, a bit of cloud, an unnoticed star. We hiked Betasso with Jim. Talked work too much and had a good time. Then home, I moved the old deck boards from under the new deck to the old slash pile. I sat on a rock and the sun cleaned me, and when I felt happy, I came in the back door. After dinner I asked her if we were doing the right things for a good life. We decided we were trying at least.

shirts drying
on the banister her hand
for balance

On Posthole Digging

Spring melt. I look at the mountain, Santoka on a string. Mountain eating. I eat mountains through eye and feets, through hands and breath. Hummingbird scramble, their ritual a heartbreak of play and muscle. Sugar on our beaks. Mountain mahogany, antelope brush, hermit thrush, this slightly sweet touch of wax currant. I'm footed, the posts four feet deep into grus earth. Mountain eating even though the sand grinds among our teeth.

the view
from white to green —
shovel hands

Hermit Chasing

I found the first traces of the Button Rock Hermit on a boulder just off of Hoof-Blaze trail. I recognized a certain scent on the air and there it was, a little buckskin pouch on top of a lichenous boulder. Inside the pouch I found a piece of crumpled paper and on it...

" — Lichen found and their Doctrines of Signature —

Rocky Mountain Sunburn - used to wind-listen and heal itches

Tiny Button Lichen - used to turn things green and clean teeth

Vagabond Lichen (far from home) - heals wanderlust and leg cramps

Cinder Lichen - burns quick and heals anger

Birch-spored Firedot - can keep you warm or cold, can spice up a juniper cone meal

Mountain Sausage Lichen - in winter, pack it into your boots for warmth; feed it to deer to learn the trails

Pale-footed Horsehair - eat it off the tree anytime

Candle Flame Lichen - if you burn it, wind will blow, but if you eat it, snow will fall

Tundra Goldspeck - if food is scarce, eat it and a rabbit will appear; heals blisters

Star-tipped Reindeer Lichen - just lick it for truth, eat it for lies"

That's all that was on the paper, that and lichen dust fingerprints.

boulder
after boulder —
i'm lost again

Fox Trail Complexities

Spike feet. The tender trail light in light snow, a hoof print, a footprint on Big Paw Peak. The forest-mind reaching in roots to my boot tread. Switchback after switchback, we know our home's depth, dark in soil heft and granite thunk. We skirt the summit regularly, not for sweat, but for sacred loneliness, for tender paths.

zig-zags
of fox trail complexities
snow in my boot

Riptime

Lateral moraine. The elk bugle and chase tail. This is riptime, between time, the rut. I scent each creature's musk. And behind us a line of clanking and morphing bones from jawtooth to brow bulge. Listen again to the wind, rain on edge and glow-sky afternoon. We spot bighorn spoor and follow hoof tracks to the riparian, fenced as it is.

wind across rocks —
explain how mountain leads
to humility

Hermit Tracking

Why Chase Hermits

Here in the foothills we wayfind with small cairns and pine knowledge. We've searched for the Button Rock Hermit through all our dreams and along all these trails but usually only see flashes of a tattered jacket and footprints on the dust and gravel. Sometimes the hermit seeps in through sap-scent and gets around our lungs, our hearts. Sometimes the hermit gets around our synapses, some soul. It's during these times that we can know why the trees creak in the calm wind and why the chickadees are brave.

flexible pine
limb tied in a knot —
why come by here

Coyote Clutch Slips

The morning in ice crystal and pine wavering with studded tires and road blood. The road ghosts frozen with snow dust. Commuter fear in the black ice and the crunch of metal and the elk grouped, steaming. The clear view far to the South, Pikes Peak, a cloud or rock. And the coyote slips her dark white coat under the barbed fence, emerging into the slow-to-wake prairie grasses.

start stop
down shift up —
white roads

Headlamps

2 AM awake. We're up strapping on all the gear for our first attempt at the summit. Two hard-boiled eggs each, three liters of water each. The trailhead crowded with headlamps, stars, true early coughs and high above us, the wind. Sweat, breath, more sweat and the layers come off in the dark, treeline lingering in dreamscapes. But breaking out, out to the crags, and I swallow hard at the vertical relief.

krummholz at dawn
far below the city
lights

On Keying Posts for a Clothesline

Brand new posthole digger. It's an old, bad joke, but I've finally got a Ph. D, honorary in its simple handle pinch and lever edge. Having never gripped or shimmed, I plunge it hard into the ground. May there be clay beneath. Sun heat and brow grit. Will this help us? Her fine thought-blood. We disagree to agree on disagreements about the tilt or key of this or that post. I dig deep for the true love of it and key the posts homestead style, pounding the board in hard with a mallet, and by late afternoon we're both smiling.

wind scorpion
tight in the dirt roots
our marriage

Overnight at Raven's Roost

The climb, of course, is difficult and it's hot in gravelly slips and solstice twist. Heavy packs, again we've brought too much for one night even after paring it down. But the new tent is light. The ravens have a nest and no one comes up here much. So quiet, it's all bug buzz and raven wing, raven croak. We hide in the cave a bit to cool off and sling up the hammock, read, write, watch clouds.

the button rock
hermit disappearing
dawn and dusk

Mitigation

The Dome, a granite outcrop towering over our small house. We climb up there to get the lay of the valley, creek meander and wildfire risk. We mitigate human desperation with hermit cave sits and hike sweat. And always, on our way down, we are ankle careful and count the epiphanies as they roll in with the rain.

one hummingbird after another our migrations

Quiet Time

When I crouched to see the beehive entrance below the branches and the flit of chickadees went and the quiet came and the crack step from the right, I saw her ears calibrate. Her smooth golden brown coat of early summer. Winter's shag all gone. Her big mule ears. Her delicate hoof step over stones and duff. Her muscles and tail twitch. As quiet as… as calm as… as alert as… And she didn't see me, smell me, hear me? My time to watch and learn.

doe stretch
over wax currant brush
time's quiet

Brush Wolf Mistress

When we began chasing the old recluse of the mountains, we didn't know what we were doing. So many wrong turns in the confusion of fox trails. So many missteps up talus slopes. We'd get to the summit and gaze out over the expanse of plains, rivers, mountain brawls, but who were we looking for? It wasn't until we stayed for a while, sipping tea and looking out at the cool, dark, north faces of the hills that we knew who we were… looking for.

mountain spirit
flying by on the wind
this giant life

Hermit Tracking

Hermit complexities. Hermit possibilities. The ancients revered their hermits for their fungi-sheathed roots that twined out into the quietude of lichen depth, old deep enigma. We writhe and shout and whine in our wifi spheres, the truth out there somewhere. Our hermits are madness and sickness and fear. It may be that we'll always be afraid of the dark: catamount lurking.

fox trail
seemingly right off

                the cliff

Beetle Grief Colorist

The slight shift of ponderosa scent. To a deep misstep in a dark but high forest. We ask folks about deep time, time the forest took to merge fungus-root to cone-seed, time for the tassel-eared squirrels to choose this or that bark. How many times have we stopped to sniff the aromatic alcohols from between pine puzzles? The Button Rock Hermit, somewhere, on some declivity, piecing bark bits together into mosaics of the Wild Hunt.

pine bark pieces
in the blue beetle grief
a wild colorist

Rituals

It never has to be
the perfect amount of time.

minutes in the woods
minutes in the meadow
seconds on the stoop

the lizard in her sun
blue-bellied
black tongue on stone

The minutes pile up
if you watch
but float off when set
beside the boulders.

Rural Cluster

Signify the mountain home. These homes with yucca yard and bare hill. I'm pleased in rock, pegmatite and quartz chunks. The grass sere and blown. Back from the dead, they said, just to die in the meadow again. And below it all, below my stone seat and stump-tilt, below my unintentional pique, the cottontail nibbles and the gas truck groans.

taken
with humanity —
grass purpose

"What's that on the wind?"

"It's the Button Rock Hermit on some far-off mountaintop yodeling to herself and innumerable clouds."

Rock Fights

Unyielding this sun winter. Not winter at all said the Jay to the Button Rock Hermit. Not autumn or spring or summer. This new season invented to irradiate fear and luck. We became inbred, somehow more white and burnt, like fox pretending at cat. We listen to rocks now and have wind fights. The bruises from stones in snowballs now black with heat. We heal and heal and cut and cut, we paint cliffs on top of columbine.

silhouette scrawl —
the moon scrapes our heads
across the snow

Daughter Fist

We found the patriarchy sitting dumbly on an icy stump. Our trigger fingers bruised enough. His torn mouth dangling. The death heat felt on cheek. The chill only life knows. "Listen," said the Jay, "turn about and descend into the sea. Your uselessness is known. The dirt-truth beckons, and I don't think you can swim. To the sea and let that blood mix with salt."

daughter fist —
the snowman's
bloody lip

Dear Hummingbird

Dear Hummingbird,

I hope all is well in the Sierra. This is what the pegmatite had to say about the human question. "The contraculture to rain is the explosion of lichen color in the theater of absurd human track, the great machismo pageantry of the self-reliant American lie. A man with beard and chainsaw is unable to love even the tiny buds who support him, unable to connect to photosynthesis because of WrestleMania. He's cloaked in his biker regalia and spits at make-up and the pageant judges but still wins best-in-show, his face unsmeared with his own fearful coming."

unimpressed the nighttime clouds move through unnoticed

Warm Regards,
The Button Rock Hermit

Deep Root Running

You! Tooth-mother,
how deep runs your tap root?
Can I recall our hike
or the number of juniper cones
ingested last memorial day,
the taste of skunk brush berries
or the spike of mountain mahogany
seeds in my pocket,
your pocket
inside-out on the descent?

The summit incants to the tooth-
mother of us,
her deep root, running.

Antler Puzzle

This thin cloud morning. In steel light, just now the tea went cold quick in camp cool air. Cold and mist. The thing, so intricate that I found last night in the doug fir hollow. The thing, a puzzle of infinite elk antlers shed in a pile so high. The thing, a toy, a hermit's incantation jam session.

morning tight
in thermal underwear —
recluse wind

Crowin' Out

Crawl to the mountainside. We heard the small dog barking at the German shepherd who was led by a German woman in crampons. The ice too cracked and stuttered our philologies. Crowologies. The hermit's French up-ended on boulder-top, dome-top overlooking the Little Elk Valley, Button Rock House just below. I see the mountain's peak, it guides us over and through and down these fox trails. We'll count the scats along the way.

crowin' out on the wind plays
        our lingua

Mind Maps

The trails of Pinewood Springs, Little Elk Park. Our mind trails. Our footpaths. Out beyond Dark Mountain, between Meadow Peak and the Slab, up Henry Trail, across the Flag Trail Traverse, around Fairyland Loop for a look at the high ranges, down Hoof-Blaze where the bones are scattered, we are just beginning. Tripping down Can-O-Worms Trail with its waterfall, down to Canyon Beach, and then right out back, Narnia Path, up to Big Paw Bench, under Fox Piss Point and Postcard, up then to the Lichen Colony and Big Pine Grove, then on up to the Dome with a bit of a scramble and Crow Feather Point. From there over above the old quarry and up to Hoarfrost Wedding where we kiss and then down to the Wind Cliffs to watch the vultures turn. Then to the Frog Ponds to wait for quiet croaks and then back across to the Bodhi Tree. Sister Rain Cave for a rest and breath. To get back to the house, Crisscross Gulch straight down or Loop-Tree-Loop for the long way around, then home with beers.

head full of names
pasque pops

Counting to Eight

From the highway we see the rack spiking up from the weeds. Old roadkill in the gully. The investigation reveals antlers, skull, spine, hide. Our desecration of the wild dead. I crank and twist until the third vertebra cracks. And I carry the rack skull and two neck bones home, beetles and rough face hides still… still… and to dry in the sun. We count both sides of the rack to eight.

my nightmare
of the wild hunt —
deer blood headlight

<u>Poems</u>

snow poems
froze
rain poems
warm
sun poems
burn
mountain poems
breath
tree poems
stick
granite poems
smooth
hermit poems
here
canyon poems
wren
river poems
slip
bear poems
shit

Hum ming bird
Poems

Buck Skull Poetics

Ungulate eater. I'm guilty and robust. I've forgiven myself and I'm complicit in all human hunts. There's no way out but to simply walk into the ponderosas and devote my life to inner-bark and lichen dust, to hermit hut. And once there, to try not to brag of my brattiness, my inability to recognize my privileges.

the deer steer clear
of the backyard buck skull —
10AM church bells

Among the Buzz

Watching thought, mind-thought, my thot. The building of mountains. The streams that build to rivers. The massive watershed of the central North American plain, dripping and my being within it, and its being cycling through multiverse unknown complexities, just as simple as the fox trail we follow to the summit of backyard Big Paw Peak, new now with a group of strangely quiet young pine squirrels. This is the now and the quiet and the real but only because there are no words for it.

figure-eight
hummingbird wing speeds—
mind sediment

Rutted

The sabbath, I pray to the cliffs. The Button Rock Hermit chants somewhere back in the pines. There is wind over everything, even the far highway roar. Our complicity sinks heart, sinks bone. I shift from reverse to first and bounce down the rutted driveway, rufous and juncos darting.

bees on the feeder
fewer hummingbirds
than yesterday

Among the Rage

The mountain's quiet pulls me in and teaches pulse, breath, and blink. The hermit said a quiet mind stays quiet even among the rage. Toothsome they say, the cave on the other side of the Wind Cliffs, and quiet too, the river.

heartbeat
slow the trout
in august

Afternoon Smoke

Tucked as I am down into the Little Tommy River Canyon box cliffs, plotting a meditation hut of stone, of stick, I scratch dry throat and eyes, dried out from rotting youth finally. The calm and slow tongue of middle age and a small pile of cap feathers. This here, that there, heavy in fruit. But fires come and flood, and the deaths of friends and the rot in tree limbs, we assess our home with nail-gun sight, and stick build our A-frame future.

scent and haze
of far wildfire
my koan cough

<u>No Journey Unworthy</u>

A few days in New Mexico. Nor New, nor Mexico, but exactly New Mexico with the brush wolf chorus and the jackrabbit hind-quarter jacked-up and a few balloon morning at Earthship tranquilo. Joy Harjo's in the distant scarlet cliffs at sunrise, and there be hermits in those old mounts too. Pilgrimage. This pilgrimage. I think there will always be a pilgrimage to New Mexico to track into the warm mornings all fox and cougar and wild yet familiar dogs, colorless and tempting. There turns out to be no journey unworthy.

sunflower tangle
bluebird exactly
teetering bluebird

Sit-Spot

There are spoor today that lead around the back of Big Paw Peak: splayed mule deer prints, fox claw-toed tracks, elk scat, black bear juniper crap. Near where the trail starts to descend through the ponderosa meadow, I stop for a sit-spot where, I believe, the brush-wolf had her sit-spot last night, overlooking Spring Gulch and the far plains. I sit and follow breath through her cycles and the wind too, Steller's Jay squawk, lizard ruffle. Letting thoughts come and go, the watching, closing the rabbit hole, opening to forest and all distance, I see how I've shut out most of life for fear of being wrong and foolish. So as the cougar opens the deer neck, I open my chest to the harsh sunlight.

smoke from wild
fires states away —
neck hairs high

Big Rock Basin

We moved to Pinewood Springs a while back.
Now it feels like forever ago.
I run wild in the hills and streams
On my days off, chasing my hermit.
There aren't many people on the trails
But wind and trees and a far off chainsaw.
I sling my hammock and watch
The clouds, listen to the chickadees.
I'm quiet and the wind howls
And the trees, they calmly creak.

Bookshelf Cut

We build it for the scent of the hot jigsaw blade through the hard oak burn, a little smoke, a little char, sawdust on the wind in my eye. We build for hand faculty, for shoulder strength, we build for a long life. We hope to build a long, calm life with warm pine air and the ice of windshield complexity.

scrolling curve cut
in the hardwood grain
our book-selves

<u>Sick Day</u>

How the boulders balance on sick day afternoons. The sun doesn't notice my razor-blade throat and the cold wind goes on its way. Hot tea. Boulder watching. Jealous clouds. Pine seduction. I could be out running in the hills! Tomorrow, after all this rest, I'll get down into some canyon and fret out my silly worries.

new fir sapling
even you know
winter wait

Hiding Hermit

Particulate

A fine morning if a little smoky. Smoke from California, smoke of distances, smoke of bone and stump, smoke of ecstasy, smoke of dry death, burnt wine. Riparian heat and cracked tooth, the Grapes of Wrath spine cracked.

wildfire
particulate —
breathe deep

Fine Young People

They're helping put the siding up.
They're measuring. Nailing.
They're looking out at the mountains,
guzzling water.
They're fine young people, speaking languages.
They're helping us.
They're sharp and lovely.
They're putting the siding up.
They're looking at mountains.

The Cruel Part and the Kind Part

Up to It's-All-Good Trail. Quiet but wind and the drip of snowmelt and the squawk of a Steller's Jay. Rock-mind, grass-mind, lichen-mind, hermit cough. Someone's voice on the wind, something urbane about the indifference of the universe, but I'm not indifferent and these hands grip sticks too.

safe at home
we do care about these
lichen movements

Solitaire Hunt

The noisy tangle of calm wildness. From the saddle of Round and Moose Mountains we count 31 ridges from tundra to plains. Our hunts typified in cloud and the shift of pine needle. Why search for hermits? Finger to lichen contact? Air to lung to tongue touch? The automobiles all far below in the canyons, race off toward the city, and we can see them, but under the sharp of this calm they are silent.

my smile on
i tuck the knife under —
mountain biker "Halloo"

Trail Knitting

The hermit's trail. An unraveling of sweater wool down through the pines, from the granite cliff, from the cave mouth or cougar maw. The paw prints in the snow clawed. We retract our statements in the blizzard's white gust, and we follow the threads to each declivity only to see the tracks again leading farther into the brush.

tangle step
through skunkbrush
mind scrapes

Sharp Decisions

Morning steps measure out in shards of hogback sandstone. Cutting, the shards make propositions impossible, each step a guarantee in the rough, abrasive, calm. Did the hermit come by here? Did she leave trace, spoor, trail? We can spot a path on the far slope and on it, a hunter's orange beanie bounces with their gait.

trailhead guess
picking out morning dreams
in foothill crux

Looking Back

yesterday's yard coyote
in my morning memory
a lost pup perhaps
somewhere up on the mountain
slope snowy
she kept looking back
and her steamy yowl

Environmental Privilege
=======================

I button my shirt up to the neck. Tie tied. I put books and lunch and keycard into my bag. I tie my shoes tight. Keys, wallet, phone. Out the door to the mountain air, pine scent, thoughts of day-off hikes. The steering wheel has its night-cold still, and the engine rumbles up. The clutch waltz. First gear to neutral coast to stop, first gear again to coast to stop at the highway. Right look, left look, first gear, second gear, third gear, the roar, fourth gear all the way down canyon. Brush wolf, mule deer, grackle. The three wild-ones rule equals our safari commute. And a strange cloud in the distance. This way to work life, mountain and town. The wildwoman-urban interface.

keyboard fingers
with wood saw callouses —
from office windows, peaks

<u>Sweater Weather</u>

We test all the different hoarfrost crystals with soft tongue. We step in dust. We find the unknown cliffs, hermit cliffs. They're shaped like mountain mind, shapely, and sharp. We nearly fall off the fog lit lichen boulders. Winter makes even the roughest granite slick. Fog burn to sun eye. On the descent we let our thumbs go cold, gripping, gripping to cunning human step.

frost needles our lips touch the intricate

Solstice Poem

I collect piles of them. The bones of all Rocky Mountain wild-ones. Stacked neatly. Windblown. Hard clank and soft crush. We pile them on the rotting stump. We stack them neatly. The bones of yard dead and roadkill, of forest kill and cougar kill. Deer colored, deer colored, stalking past our stump bones.

solstice eve —
i tilt the deer skull
just so

Winter Ascent

The dark crunch. The light slip. The snowpack. Gaiters for post-holing up through the krummholz. Yin haunted trees, we worship their root dark. Bones of wood bent and alone. We cough in the deep night, and then light cracks. Sun still black, sun still cold. Hermit frost. The wind yawns up out of canyon dawn. And our ascent to the ice rock goes on.

depth hoar —
ice in ice facets
of our faces

Hermit Hut

We come upon the hut by luck. She says, "What's that pile of sticks?" We descend the declivity, and she says, "There's a hole, an entrance." The pile is a home, a hut, with barbed wire lashings. Once inside, with a whistle, we see enough in the dark, stone seats, stump table, shelves of branch with jars full of small wild wonders, jars of teeth, beetles, grus, spider legs, deep liquids, mosses, seeds, bone fragments, flower petals, jars of roots, each labeled with words of stick-built letters shaped into canopies and cliff-sides, and wild-ones. "Is this her hut," she says, "the hut of the Button Rock Hermit, the Root Weaver?" But we have no answers, only fear. So we leave that place and continue to the summit.

a single painting
of a city street —
these bones, teeth

Tooth and Tongue

The night's shade. I pop the cherry tomato into my mouth and burst it with tooth and tongue. The night shades that swarm in spirits out the back door window in deep woods dark. Out there she moves quiet, and the deer murmur and her claws retract once in the duff. Pine needle snaps. Me and my tomato crunch and she and her neck vertebra crack among tooth and tongue.

cougar print
in old snow
drops of blood

Complicit with Our Heat

Cloud sink to 7000'. House level. Home elevation. Snow inches. We, in oneiric mist, forecast the millimeters of black ice. The studded tires wear at a rate complicit with our heat, and our bodies, as animal as they are, move as automatons through the yucca spines, the bayonets, through the snow dust. The hermit watches from somewhere up in the boulders with her own meteorology lined-up.

my snowball
crumbles in mid-air
our humidity

Threadless

Light dry snow. The fog blows through in cloud out cloud. The sun somewhere. Post-burn krummholz. We're illicit on the ground. Wrong primates. The future recedes daily, and we count the pine needles in preparation for the smallest of small basket weaves, threadless and brittle.

thought fragments
the snow drifts on top
of them all

This Ecotone

We're tooth bitten. We're our own professors of cruelty. As giant trucks carrying juiced food jake-brake down wooded mountain canyons, as the toothless chew with blood gums, as they crack open human canker, in blood blister, to see black.

this cut-word
of foothill ecotone —
desert fingers curl

Mistake Mountain

We grew up in the hollers of the eastern mountains, but I never thought we'd live in mountains. The wind is terrifying. The snow endless. And the ice of mountains. We came here with nothing but packs, unhoused. The pines stood, the boulders sat, the creeks ran, the hermits hid in mountains. Now, we look at mountains and think of Santoka with his hat, think of snow and rain and mountains.

ice banners
off the roof eaves —
all our mis-takes

That Cloud

The same cloud lingers over Button Rock, pink in the morning, gray in the afternoon, black in the hermit-shine moon. How long we remain. And today the new power lines are going up. Hard hat people. Their work clunks around and the deer stare. Their work clunks around and the crows burst. Their work clunks around. The cloud seems to move but doesn't. It lingers for days and then one morning it will just be gone.

each day
a few new birds —
wanderlust

Torpor Release

All loose as the wet ground swells to sense. All toothy the torpor release. All consuming the red and yellow of blood and tendon. Mouth water. We tip-toe through thick duff and across mossy pads. We stop, for our bodies have sensed something we yet know not. And the bear sees us only after and bursts away through the juniper thicket never once looking back.

just the nips
of the hedgehog cactus buds
we stick out

A Shift of Tree Talk

In the foothills even the smallest changes come on big and windy. We walk all around the crags and forests, we heave up through all the gulches, all the gullies. We count deer, track bobcats, eat juniper cones. And as we breathe it all out, we sense, ever so slightly, a shift in the tree talk, and we know someone is watching.

not so much different hermit path dust

Hermit Sniffing

we crept into your ink mountains
we liked counting fog ridges
and soon smelled that they were
smoke ridges
we stumbled into your ink mountains
got our fingers stuck together
got our feet wet in dry creeks
got our tongues caught and twisted
the hermit whispering her lichen
spell over our shroomed, midnight
owl eyes
the voles
below
sniffing

Hiding Hermit

River hike. Up and over the rapids, through them, hip deep. Snails detach and float by, relocation. The clear and deep. Minnows school-out, the shape of current and cool. We slip in step, hiking poles tapping through submerged granite, grus and tangle. Did you see that movement on the high ridgeline, a face, a leg, an ear twitch. We listen for the incantation but only the sun howls and our zinc coated skin slips in and out of water.

merganser
hen floof and cluck
ducklings hiding hermit

Acknowledgements

Some of these poems have appeared in *Beats: Writing from A Place of Urgency*, *Contemporary Haibun Online*, *Haibun Today*, and *Ink, Sweat, and Tears*.

Before Scott King of Red Dragonfly Press passed away, he graciously awarded the manuscript for this book the Meadowhawk Prize. Working with him for the short time that I did was an honor. He will be remembered fondly, and the works that he helped put into the world will continue to influence me and many others.

About the Author

Tony Burfield has had his poetry published in *Contemporary Haibun Online, Beats: Writing from A Place of Urgency, The Heron's Nest, Lilliput Review, Ink, Sweat, and Tears* and *Modern Haiku*. His collection of haibun, *Sawhorse,* won the 2017 Fledge Poetry Chapbook Award. He lives with his wife in Pinewood Springs, CO and works at the Boulder Public Library.

About Middle Creek Publishing

MIDDLE CREEK PUBLISHING believes that responding to the world through art & literature — and sharing that response — is a vital part of being an artist.

MIDDLE CREEK PUBLISHING is a company seeking to make the world a better place through both the means and ends of publishing. We are publishers of quality literature in any genre from authors and artists, both seasoned and as-yet undervalued, with a great interest in works which may be considered to be, illuminate or embody any aspect of contemplative Human Ecology, defined as the relationship between humans and their natural, social, and built environments.

MIDDLE CREEK's particular interest in Human Ecology, is meant to clarify an aspect of the quality in the works we will consider for publication, and is meant as a guide to those considering submitting work to us. Our interest is in publishing works illuminating the Human experience through words, story or other content that connects us to each other, our environment, our history, and our potential deeply and more consciously.

www.ingramcontent.com/pod-product-compliance
Lightning Source LLC
Chambersburg PA
CBHW062118080426
42734CB00012B/2905